THE STORY OF CASSIOPEIA

A ROMAN CONSTELLATION MYTH

A RETELLING BY
THOMAS KINGSLEY TROUPE

ILLUSTRATED BY
ROBERT SQUIER

PICTURE WINDOW BOOKS
a capstone imprint

Look into the night sky, and you'll see clusters of stars. They're called constellations. Each of the 88 constellations tells a story. This story of Queen Cassiopeia comes from ancient Rome.

Queen Cassiopeia and King Cepheus ruled a kingdom
called Ethiopia. The people of Ethiopia loved the royal family.
They were very excited when Princess Andromeda was born.
Soon the princess had grown into a beautiful young woman.

Cassiopeia loved her daughter, and she loved her own beauty too. Cassiopeia would often say to the people of her kingdom, "My daughter and I are quite beautiful, aren't we?" The people of Ethiopia would always agree.

One day Cassiopeia boasted, "We are both even more beautiful than the sea nymphs." Little did she know the sea nymphs had overheard.

The nymphs were angered by Cassiopeia's words. They swam to tell their father, Neptune.

"Cassiopeia is not a god. She should not say such things!" Neptune shouted. He decided to talk to Jupiter, the most powerful god.

Jupiter was shocked. "She believes she is even more beautiful than the nymphs?" he asked. "Teach her a lesson!"

Neptune called for the mighty sea monster, Cetus.
"Flood Ethiopia until nothing is left!" roared Neptune.
"Cassiopeia will pay for her boast!"

But Cetus wasn't the only one to hear Neptune's
order. In a nearby boat, a sailor had heard everything.

The man quickly sailed to shore. He ran to the king to tell him the news.

King Cepheus turned to his wife after hearing the story. "You've doomed us all!" he yelled.

Queen Cassiopeia looked out at the rising waves. She was sorry for what she had said.

The king knew there was little time. He went to the Oracle for advice. "How can I win over the gods?" he asked. "They want to destroy us all for Cassiopeia's words."

"You must offer your beautiful daughter to the sea monster," the Oracle said. "Only then will the gods spare you and your people."

The king was stunned. How could he
send his only daughter to die?

With no other choice, King Cepheus left
to do as the Oracle had said.

13

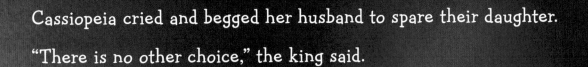

Cassiopeia cried and begged her husband to spare their daughter.

"There is no other choice," the king said.

Cassiopeia said good-bye to her beautiful daughter. Then King Cepheus took Andromeda to a seaside cliff. With tears in his eyes, he chained her to the cliff wall.

"Father," Andromeda cried. "There must be another way!"

The king kissed his daughter's forehead. He loved her. But he had to save his kingdom and his people.

As the monster Cetus rose from the sea,
giant waves rolled toward the kingdom.

The princess looked at Cetus and screamed.

A brave hero named Perseus heard Andromeda's cries. When he saw the beautiful princess, he knew he had to save her. Perseus had a plan.

Perseus flew his horse, Pegasus, close to Cetus. When he was near enough, he pulled the monster Medusa's head from his bag. Snakes twisted on her head. Anyone who looked at Medusa turned to stone.

Cetus tried to strike Perseus. But Perseus turned quickly, holding out Medusa's head. Just then, Cetus looked right at Medusa. He instantly turned to stone.

Perseus freed the princess and returned her to the castle.
King Cepheus and Queen Cassiopeia were overjoyed.

"How can I ever repay you?" the king asked.

"Your Majesty, I would like to marry your daughter,"
answered Perseus.

Perseus and Andromeda were soon married. Everyone in the kingdom was happy for them—even the gods.

In time the gods raised King Cepheus, Queen Cassiopeia, Andromeda, and Perseus into the sky as constellations. But the gods did not forget Cassiopeia's selfishness. As punishment, Cassiopeia's constellation appears upside down most of the time.

Night sky from the northern half of Earth in fall

LEARN MORE

For as long as people have lived, stories have been told about the constellations. Cassiopeia's constellation can be seen in the northern sky year-round. The five stars make up a "W" shape, representing Cassiopeia's throne. The formation of King Cepheus sparkles just above of his queen.

Just below Cassiopeia, the constellations Andromeda and Perseus can be found. A bit to the right, the winged horse Pegasus shines in the night sky.

In Chinese astronomy, a formation called Wang Liang is part of Cassiopeia's constellation. The star group celebrates a legendary Chinese man who rode a chariot. A line of four stars is meant to be the horses. The fifth star is Wang Liang himself.

CAST OF CHARACTERS

Cassiopeia—queen of Ethiopia; mother of Andromeda

Cepheus—king of Ethiopia; father of Andromeda

Andromeda—princess of Ethiopia; daughter of Cassiopeia and Cepheus

sea nymphs—beautiful young maidens who live in the sea; children of Neptune

Neptune—god of the sea; brother of Jupiter and Pluto

Jupiter—god of sky and thunder and king of the gods

Cetus—a sea monster sent by Neptune to destroy Ethiopia

Oracle—a priestess who could tell people about events in the future

Perseus—a hero who killed the monster Medusa and saves Andromeda from Cetus

Pegasus—a flying horse that Perseus rides upon

Medusa—a monster with a head of living snakes who turns creatures to stone when they look at her

GLOSSARY

astronomy—the study of stars, planets, and other objects in space

chariot—a two-wheeled vehicle, often pulled by horses

constellation—a group of stars that forms a shape

legendary—something or someone that is part of a story handed down from earlier times

nymph—a mythical maiden on a mountain, in a forest, or in a body of water

READ MORE

Kim, F. S. *Constellations*. A True Book. New York: Children's Press, 2010.

Mitton, Jacqueline. *Once Upon a Starry Night: A Book of Constellation Stories*. Washington, D. C.: National Geographic, 2003.

Rustad, Martha E. H., *The Stars*. Out in Space. Mankato, Minn.: Capstone Press, 2009.

INTERNET SITES

FactHound offers a safe, fun way to find Internet sites related to this book. All of the sites on FactHound have been researched by our staff.

Here's all you do:

Visit *www.facthound.com*

Type in this code: 9781404873766

Super-cool stuff! Check out projects, games and lots more at www.capstonekids.com

LOOK FOR ALL THE BOOKS IN
THE NIGHT SKY STORIES SERIES:

FOLLOW THE
DRINKING GOURD

THE STORY OF **CASSIOPEIA**

THE STORY OF **ORION**

THE STORY OF **URSA MAJOR**
AND **URSA MINOR**

Thanks to our advisers for their expertise, research, and advice:
David Burgess
District #77 Planetarium Director, Mankato, Minnesota

Terry Flaherty, PhD, Professor of English
Minnesota State University, Mankato

Editor: Shelly Lyons
Designer: Alison Thiele
Art Director: Nathan Gassman
Production Specialist: Danielle Ceminsky
The illustrations in this book were created digitally.

Picture Window Books
1710 Roe Crest Drive
North Mankato, Minnesota 56003
877-845-8392
www.capstonepub.com

Library of Congress Cataloging-in-Publication Data
Troupe, Thomas Kingsley.
  The story of Cassiopeia: a Roman constellation myth: a retelling / by Thomas Kingsley Troupe ; illustrations by Robert Squier.
    p. cm. — (Capstone picture window books. Night sky stories)
  Includes index.
  ISBN 978-1-4048-7376-6 (library binding)
  ISBN 978-1-4048-7716-0 (paperback)
  ISBN 978-1-4048-7988-1 (eBook PDF)
  1. Stars—Juvenile literature. 2. Cassiopeia (Constellation)—Juvenile literature. 3. Mythology, Roman—Juvenile literature. I. Squier, Robert, ill. II. Title.

QB801.7.T76 2013
398.20937—dc23   2012001247

Printed in the United States of America in North Mankato, Minnesota.
042012   006682CGF12